Giggles for the Gals
WHEN YOU NEED A POETICALLY PRESCRIBED PICK ME UP

ALEX DEMPSEY

I present you with a chapbook that focuses on the lighter side of poetry. This chapbook is packed with comedy, warmth and relatable poems, written with you in mind.

Copyright © 2024 by Alex Dempsey

All rights reserved.

No part of this book may be reproduced in any form or by any electronic or mechanical means, including information storage and retrieval systems, without written permission from the author, except for the use of brief quotations in a book review.

For my Family

Contents

1. Online Dating — 1
2. Shopping on a Saturday — 3
3. The Hairdressers — 5
4. The Truth about Getting Old — 7
5. Living with a Man — 9
6. Nightclub Bathroom: Questions You are Likely to Hear — 11
7. The Drunk Auntie at Christmas — 13
8. Dad's Introduction to Code Red — 15
9. One of those Days — 18
10. Dieting Isn't for Me — 20
11. Driving Sucks — 22
12. Live Real Life — 24
13. Just Your Average Office Job — 26
14. Swimming — 29
15. The Morning After the Night Before — 32
16. The Afternoon After the Night Before — 35

Acknowledgments — 39
About the Author — 41

Online Dating

I sent a smiley face,
And now he's imitating,
What on earth do I reply to that?
I hate online dating.

They ask you too many questions,
It's far too suffocating,
'Where are you and what are you up to?'
I hate online dating.

I can't keep up with the conversations,
It's incredibly frustrating,
'Are you Steve or Tom, from Greece or West Brom?'
I hate online dating.

I don't want to message forever,
I don't need a pen pal from Beijing,
But I don't want to meet you after two messages,
I hate online dating.

ALEX DEMPSEY

I have a broken ankle,
And he wants us to go ice-skating,
It's not often I'm speechless,
I hate online dating.

I don't want to see his phallus,
And I have zero interest in mating,
If he thinks it turns us on, he's oh so wrong,
I hate online dating.

Shopping on a Saturday

'Good afternoon Madam,
How can I help you today?'
Bog off and leave me alone,
Is what I really wanted to say.

I replied to the retail assistant,
'I'm just looking thank you,'
Flashed her a grimace,
And plodded on through.

I was in a bad mood,
Before I'd walked through the door,
And with the sight of the crowds,
The mood worsened some more.

My eyes were drawn to a lonely blouse,
It was a beautiful shade of blue,
But on the hanger it said size twelve,
And inside it said size twenty-two.

ALEX DEMPSEY

I put the blouse back,
And carried on around the floor,
I wouldn't have done so however,
If I knew what was in store.

I needed to take my jumper off,
As it was unbearably muggy,
And while the jumper was over my head,
I was rammed into by a buggy.

Not so much as an apology,
Nor a question to ask if I was okay,
But that's quite alright,
Who needs their heels anyway?

I flung my shoes off in a rage,
And hobbled over to the nearest seat,
Sat down without looking,
And sat on a sticky boiled sweet.

I flicked it off and looked at my heels,
Just wallowing in the disaster,
I looked inside my handbag,
And do you think I could find a plaster?

As I shuffled to the exit,
To make my getaway,
I told myself to never again,
Go shopping on a Saturday.

The Hairdressers

As I look around the salon,
From my hydraulic swivel chair,
There is more on my mind,
Than how I want my hair.

Everybody looks so glamorous,
The clients and the staff,
I wonder if they look at me,
And have a little laugh.

I'm bare faced and wearing sweats,
So I will allow for some jest,
And under the fluorescent lights,
I know no one looks like their best.

How long should I wait,
Before I ask for a cup of tea?
Do I tell her how I like it,
Or do I wait for her to ask me?

ALEX DEMPSEY

The small talk questions are the worst,
'Have you had a nice day?'
'What do you do for work again?'
'Do you have plans to go away?'

'I'm just here for the head massage,
When does it take place?'
Deep slow circles over the scalp,
And gentle strokes to the face.

How do I politely say no,
To reading their Salon's magazine?
By the looks of it,
It hasn't been read or wiped since 1918.

I don't want to be difficult,
But if the water gets too hot,
Or if the water gets in my eyes,
Should I let her know or not?

If I don't like my hair,
Do I pretend that I do?
Unless my hair falls out,
Then I might have to sue.

When I leave today,
And I head over to the till,
I wonder if the quote,
Will finally match the bill.

The Truth about Getting Old

You know you're getting old,
When nothing's fun anymore,
When you struggle to remember,
What you did the night before.

You know you're getting old,
When you ask people to shout,
When you giggle just a little,
And a lot of wee comes out.

You know you're getting old,
When you're roots come through grey,
When you can hear yourself repeating,
The same things every day.

You know you're getting old,
When your brain is getting slower,
When you've got decking in your garden,
But you've been looking for a mower.

ALEX DEMPSEY

You know you're getting old,
When you can't hear the telly,
When your belly's on your knees,
And your boobs are on your belly.

You know you're getting old,
When you can't move freely anymore,
When you can't get up,
After sitting on the floor.

You know you're getting old,
When you're someone's Nan or Nanny,
When there's more hair on your chin,
Than there is on your fanny.

Living with a Man

Living with a man,
Ain't all it's cracked up to be,
I have to put the toilet seat down,
After he's been for a pee.

Living with a man,
Ain't all it's cracked up to be,
He never pairs his socks up,
So we lose them daily.

Living with a man,
Ain't all it's cracked up to be,
When I ask why the chores haven't been done,
He just smiles at me.

Living with a man,
Ain't all it's cracked up to be,
Even when I'm cold,
The heating isn't allowed to move above twenty.

ALEX DEMPSEY

Living with a man,
Ain't all it's cracked up to be,
He has selective hearing,
But then says 'you never told me!'

Living with a man,
Ain't all it's cracked up to be,
I can't always watch Eastenders,
Because football seems to take priority.

Living with a man,
Ain't all it's cracked up to be,
I wash his clothes and dirty undies,
And see things a wife shouldn't see.

Nightclub Bathroom: Questions You are Likely to Hear

Could you please hold that?
Does my bum look big in this?
Where did you get your dress from?
When did you have your first kiss?
Does anyone have any toilet roll?
Do you feel alright?
Have you messaged him back?
Are you out for the night?
Do you want to share a cubicle?
Where did I put my phone?
Do you want a tequila or sambuca shot?
Do you listen to Post Malone?
Are you still going to cry over him?
Do you really give a damn?
Do you fancy meeting up tomorrow?
Can I follow you on Instagram?
Where are you going after here?
Do you have any body spray?

ALEX DEMPSEY

Please could I have some chewing gum?
Did you even like her anyway?

The Drunk Auntie at Christmas

As I polished off a bottle of red,
And started on the brandy,
It suddenly dawned on me,
That I was the drunk Auntie.

The drunk Auntie at Christmas,
Who falls into the tree,
And starts a fight with anyone,
Who tries to stop the party.

The drunk Auntie at Christmas,
Who forgets what gift she got you,
It's not only a surprise for the recipient,
But the present giver too.

The drunk Auntie at Christmas,
Who barely touches the grub,
Who would rather drink and dance,
And pretend to be in a nightclub.

The drunk Auntie at Christmas,
Who wears a low cut top,
And gets wolf whistled at,
As she's picking up cigs and wine at the Co-op.

The drunk Auntie at Christmas,
Who gets hassled by Nanny Lou,
'Are you still single,
Because there's something wrong with you?'

The drunk Auntie at Christmas,
Who retaliates back to Nanny Lou,
'There is nothing wrong with me,
And it will happen when it's meant to.'

The drunk Auntie at Christmas,
Who wakes up with her limbs akimbo,
Hanging upside down off the sofa,
Wondering what the hell happened to Crimbo!

Dad's Introduction to Code Red

Wouldn't it be nice,
If men had a clue,
What a period felt like,
And what us women went through?

I was caught out on the loo once,
And I shouted to my Dad,
'Please could you do me a favour,
And fetch me a tampon or a pad?'

Dad shouted back to me,
'Get it yourself,
I think they're in the cabinet,
Above the bath and on the top shelf.'

He was sadly mistaken,
If he thought I could stretch,
I was curled up like a sleeping cat,
Trying my hardest not to wretch.

ALEX DEMPSEY

'Dad, I need you!'
'Dad!' I shouted once more,
'You will need to come and help me,
Unless you want blood on the floor!'

He eventually came up,
Tutting and grumbling,
'You're such a wimp,'
I heard him mumbling.

He flailed around in the basket,
Not knowing what was where,
So I asked him to pass me,
A blue padded square.

'Thank you very much,
For getting me my supplies,'
I reached out towards the pad,
And he closed his eyes.

I have never seen my Dad,
Run so fast before,
No sooner than I had blinked,
He had bolted out the door.

I'm not sure if he was scared,
Of what he might see,
Or if he was just embarrassed,
Not knowing how to help me.

I don't think he expected me,
To be in so much pain,
I was sweating and grimacing,

And using God's name in vain.

I know it wasn't nice for him,
To see me in that state,
But he'd rather me have a period,
Than have the worry when it's late!

One of those Days

Have you ever had one of those days,
Where you should've just stayed in bed?

I wasted a good ten minutes,
Looking for the glasses on my head,
Which annoyed me slightly,
As I could've spent those in bed.

I was jogging towards the bus,
As I was already late,
And then the heavens opened,
Leaving me in a right old soggy state.

I got to work eventually,
And realised I hadn't packed my lunch,
And even my emergency snack drawer,
Was out of things to munch.

I went down to the restaurant,

And bought a salad and a bubble tea,
I tripped over my laces,
And threw it all over the man behind me.

'I'm so sorry, Sir,
Please can you forgive me somehow?'
I said while grabbing his tie,
And mopping his brow.

'Don't worry my lovely,
It's not your fault,
I'm glad you didn't go for the chips,
I can't stand the taste of salt!'

We had a laugh together,
And then I went on my way,
To finish my shift,
And say goodbye to today.

I left work an hour early,
And I'm not even sorry,
I needed to get out of my wet clothes,
Have a red wine and watch Corrie.

Corrie was cancelled,
And I dropped the bottle of merlot,
So I took it as a sign to hit the hay,
And start afresh tomorrow.

Today was one of those days,
I should've just stayed in bed.

Dieting Isn't for Me

Why do we get so fixated,
On how much we weigh?
And why do we find ourselves waiting,
To start the 'diet' next Monday?

Who wants to be counting calories,
And recording every 'point' and 'syn?'
I know when I've been eating too much,
Because I've grown an extra chin.

Somewhere you will read,
'An avocado contains healthy fat,'
And elsewhere you will hear,
'An avocado is calorific, don't eat that.'

Diets can be so conflicting,
And it causes me added stress,
I get so worn out trying to plan my meals,
That I end up in a mess.

I've heard one trillion times,
To flush the fat away,
You must drink at least eight cups of water,
Every single day.

I've tried and failed miserably,
But is that what people do?
Force themselves to drink tasteless liquid,
And spend most of the day on the loo?

When I'm not following a diet plan,
I tell myself that I'm going to be 'good,'
But I restrict myself for far too long,
And end up eating more than I should.

If you want to go on a diet,
Go girl! You reach that goal,
Everyone should feel happy,
In their skin and in their soul.

I'm finished with 'dieting,'
I think balance is key,
Eating a jam donut while walking to work,
Is a happy balance for me.

Driving Sucks

Does anyone else suck at driving,
Or is it just me?
The only reason I do it,
Is to get from A to B.

I only got three minors,
On my first ever driving test,
So surely I can't be that bad,
I know I'm not the best?

I passed my driving test,
Ten years ago this year,
And when I offer my taxi services,
Friends still look at me with fear.

I'm not very good at street parking,
And this I will admit,
I can't tell if the space is big enough,
So I just hope my car will fit.

GIGGLES FOR THE GALS

I get anxious when it doesn't,
As I watch the lineup of cars grow,
Street parking for me,
Is just a big fat no.

Roundabouts are the worst,
I can never understand the signs,
I end up panicking and find it hard,
To stay in between the lines.

I stopped on a roundabout once,
And that was a huge mistake,
I didn't mean to though,
I missed the clutch and tapped the brake.

If you catch me on a roundabout,
You are best to avoid this mess,
Roundabouts make me question,
If I should've stayed a passenger princess.

Thinking about it now,
I'm lucky I'm not dead,
And maybe I should look at getting,
A bicycle instead.

Live Real Life

Look up at the stars,
And see them twinkle in the sky.
Go to see a stand-up comic,
And laugh until you cry.
Ride the fastest roller coaster,
And eat candy floss at the fair.
Change the cut or colour,
Or the style of your hair.
Go to your favourite charity shop,
And grab yourself a cheap buy.
Arrange to meet up with an old friend,
And watch time fly.
Absorb the elated atmosphere,
After watching a stage show.
Absorb the happiness you feel,
Watching re-runs and drinking prosecco.
Drive around in the summer,
With your windows wound down.
Watch trapeze artists at the circus,

And get a photo with a clown.
Partake in a night class,
Or try a new activity.
Go travelling while you can,
If you have the ability.
Sing as loud as you can,
At a concert or in the car.
Write a heartfelt letter to someone,
Letting them know how special they are.
Live in the moment,
And put your mobile phone away.
Enjoy the real things,
And live for today!

Just Your Average Office Job

I see zombies with their black coffee,
Every single morning,
I see them hiding behind their mugs,
Trying to hide their mouths while yawning.

A caffeine fix is imperative,
To get you through the nine to five,
I have three or four during the day,
It's the only way to survive.

The repetitive nature of my job,
Makes me want to scream and yelp,
'Hello you're through to an administrator,
How can I help?'

'This needs to be finished,
By the close of play,'
Is a phrase heard in our office,
At least three times a day.

GIGGLES FOR THE GALS

'With the best will in the world,'
Is another phrase too,
Along with 'let's touch base,'
And 'I'll just ping this over to you.'

Karen is our office manager,
And a Karen she is indeed,
If she ever cut herself,
Excel and Word are all she would bleed.

Only ever working in this job,
I think since time began,
Is the fun sponge of the office,
So I try my best to avoid Roxanne.

Roxanne can be hard to notice,
As she is quite a bit smaller,
I have to make stealth like moves,
When I need a drink from the water cooler.

If I make it to the water cooler,
I am guaranteed to meet Helen there,
She is the gossipmonger,
Who knows who, what, when and where.

I don't know how she does it,
But she seems to know it all,
I am beginning to wonder,
If under her desk is a crystal ball.

The smokers of the office,
Have two intervals a day,
Not including their lunch breaks,

ALEX DEMPSEY

How is that fair in any way?

I can't be the only one either,
Who sits at their desk and thinks,
I wish Karen, Bob and Scott knew,
Just how much cigarette smoke stinks.

Scott wears his clothes too tight,
And has putrid smelling breath,
I would rather date the Grim Reaper,
And take my chances with death.

Along with the rest of the office,
Scott has asked me out before,
He is twice my age and lives with an 'ex,'
Scott is the office man-whore.

Every Friday night,
I treat myself to a scotch,
I look back on the working week,
And it's always worth the watch.

Swimming

I find swimming so relaxing,
But I find the process quite a faff,
Parking isn't always easy,
And the changing rooms are naff.

The beige tiles on the floor are filthy,
A right unsightly state,
You can almost see the verrucas,
Just lying there in wait.

The showers aren't any better,
They are completely caked in mould,
And they only have two temperatures,
Scalding hot and freezing cold.

I haven't liked my body,
Since the age of seventeen,
And the cubicles that are useable,
Are few and far between.

To use their broken lockers,
They try to charge you 20p,
But out of principal I just say,
'Sorry, I don't have change with me.'

There's enough to remember already,
And you are packed to the rafters,
Making sure you've got everything,
For the beginning, middle and afters.

If they were electronically secured,
And were working as they should be,
I wouldn't have to try and remember,
To bring a padlock with me.

Once I've finished my swim,
And I'm dressed and pristine,
I always take a cheeky trip,
To the vending machine.

Those laps around the pool,
I have to say,
Make my body really crave,
A packet of crisps and a Milky Way.

The last time I went swimming,
My blonde hair turned green,
So I had to counteract the reaction,
Between the copper and chlorine.

Thank heavens for the internet,
I knew what I needed to do,
And that was to bathe my hair in a mixture,

Of baking soda and shampoo.

It was a simple fix,
And I'm so very grateful for that,
But now I don't dare enter the pool,
Without wearing a swimming hat.

The Morning After the Night Before

As my blood shot eyes open,
I feel half dead,
I roll over to a half eaten kebab,
And garlic mayonnaise in the bed.

It takes all of my might,
To hold in my spew,
But I refuse to get out of my pit,
Unless it's to use the loo.

I need to get into my pyjamas,
And get out of this dress,
I would jump in the shower,
But there's no cleaning up this mess.

I was definitely wearing tights,
When I left the house last night,
And as I lay looking up at the ceiling,
I see them wrapped around the light.

GIGGLES FOR THE GALS

I have no idea what happened,
Or how they ended up there,
All I know right now is,
That I am far too hungover to care.

How can I get home at the crack of dawn,
When I left the house at dusk?
And why do I have vague memories,
Of waving my card around like I'm Elon Musk.

I won't be looking at my online banking,
Anytime soon that's for sure,
I will need to look for my handbag though,
I think I threw it on the floor.

I not only lose my memory,
But over time I've lost many things,
A driving license, four phones,
Countless lipsticks and Thomas Sabo earrings.

I'm feeling rather sick,
I need to open the windows,
And I'm now seriously regretting,
Pre-ordering a Domino's.

I haven't looked at my phone yet,
It fills me with absolute dread,
What if I've pissed off a friend,
With something that I've said?

I will look at my phone later,
And I will be declining every tag request,
I only have photos on my social media,

Where I look nothing but my best.

Why do we take so many photos?
Snap...Snap...Snap,
We only like them until we're sober,
Another reason I dread opening WhatsApp.

I don't want to see,
That I've drunk dialled my ex,
It wouldn't be the first time,
I've drunkenly called him for sex.

Why do I get so drunk?
I am feeling nothing but regret,
Was last night one to remember,
Or was it one to forget?

The Afternoon After the Night Before

I pulled back the covers,
And jumped out of bed,
I went downstairs for an ice cold drink,
To clear this wooly head.

I poured a glass from the carton,
And the remainder down my throat,
Alcohol being the poison,
And orange juice being the antidote.

I strolled into the living room,
And flopped down on the settee,
After fetching a blanket,
My phone and remote for the TV.

I started watching a psychological thriller,
It was called 'The Head,'
But I found that I needed an easy watch,
So put on 'Four in a bed.'

ALEX DEMPSEY

I looked behind me at the clock,
And I started to swoon,
My appetite was coming back,
And Domino's would be here soon.

I hadn't looked at my phone,
In oh so long,
But time was getting on,
And I needed to put right any wrong.

As I went through my apps,
My tentative frown,
Rather quickly,
Turned upside down.

All that was in my inbox,
Was an unread message 'Where are you?'
And my sent box was empty,
So I let out a 'phew!'

I had taken 35 photos,
And I smiled at every single one,
Looking back on the night out,
We sure had some fun.

I was expecting more than 35 photos,
It seemed a little light,
But I'm guessing my battery died,
Half way through the night.

Maybe I was just too busy,
Happy in the zone,
Dancing, singing and laughing,

GIGGLES FOR THE GALS

To think about my phone.

I will stick to wine in the future,
And won't mix it with beer,
That is honestly a lesson learned,
The hangover was far too severe.

They say 'you're only young once,'
And that is obviously true,
Does this saying count however,
When you're 42?

Acknowledgments

I would like to express my sincere gratitude and appreciation to Robert 'Bob' Harrison at Seneca Author Services. Bob's assistance, support and indispensable knowledge during the book making process, has truly been invaluable.

Bob provided a wealth of knowledge and was an absolute pleasure to communicate with.

I am extremely grateful to him for his time and effort in helping me to achieve my goal and produce my first poetry chapbook.

I would also like to thank my family and friends for their assistance and continued support.

I am beyond grateful to have the support network that I do and I will be forever grateful for the continual encouragement that I am given, to follow my dreams.

Thank you for reading.

Sincerely,
  Alex

About the Author

Alex Dempsey (was Robinson) is a wife to Owen and has two furbabies, Buddy and Ronnie. Alex is a kind and caring individual who works in administration at her local Hospital.

Alex particularly enjoys the simple things in life such as; spending time with family and friends, writing poetry and drinking tea.

Alex particularly dislikes inequality, walking over bridges and olives.

As well as this chapbook, Alex also has a children's poetry book currently going through the illustration process.

During the course of growing up, Alex has always had an avid interest in creative writing especially poetry and has now found the courage to unleash her creativity and charm upon the world.

Please follow Alex on her Instagram account for the latest updates and to get an added insight into Alex's witty world: @poetrybyalexd

Please also remember to #bekind

Printed in Great Britain
by Amazon